TAVISTOCK TO PLYMOUTH

Vic Mitchell and Keith Smith

MP *Middleton Press*

Cover picture: Class T9 no. 30709 climbs the 1 in 75 north of Bere Alston with the 10.2am Plymouth to Waterloo on 12th May 1961. On the right is the Calstock Viaduct which carried trains to Callington at that time. (S.C.Nash)

First Published November 1996
Reprinted May 1999

ISBN 1 873793 88 X

© Middleton Press, 1996

Design Deborah Goodridge

Published by
        Middleton Press
        Easebourne Lane
        Midhurst, West Sussex
        GU29 9AZ
Tel: 01730 813169
Fax: 01730 812601

Printed & bound by Biddles Ltd,
        Guildford and Kings Lynn

CONTENTS

ACKNOWLEDGEMENTS

We are very appreciative of the help received from so many of those mentioned in the photographic credits and also for that given by R.Carpenter, G.Croughton, M.J.Furnell, P.Hay, M.King, N.Langridge, J.S.Petley, Mr D. & Dr S.Salter, P.Shaw, M.Turvey, E.Youldon and our ever helpful wives.

GEOGRAPHICAL SETTING

At Tavistock the route was on the north side of the deep valley of the River Tavy and it crossed three of its tributaries before transferring to the valley of the River Tamar at Bere Alston. South thereof the track remains in use and descends to the tidal shore of the Tamar, near its confluence with the Tavy. It crosses the latter on a curved viaduct and continues parallel to the Tamar before entering the western suburbs of Plymouth.

A sinuous undulating course took trains through the city to the Friary terminus in its southeast district. Connections to the many docks and Naval establishments were once of commercial and strategic importance.

The Callington branch dropped steeply from Bere Alston to cross the Tamar Valley on a tall viaduct to enter Cornwall at Calstock. Thereafter it climbs sharply to its present terminus at Gunnislake. The line rose further before descending to the final station which was near the village of Kelly Bray. This section of the route traversed an area where granite was quarried and copper, tin, silver and arsenic were once mined. The main line was largely on limestone and slate of no economic importance.

Maps are to the scale of 25 ins to 1 mile, unless otherwise stated.

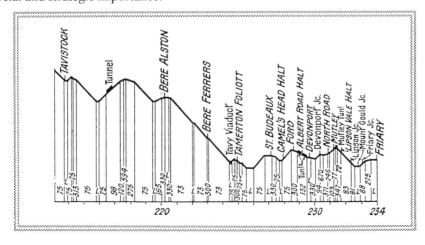

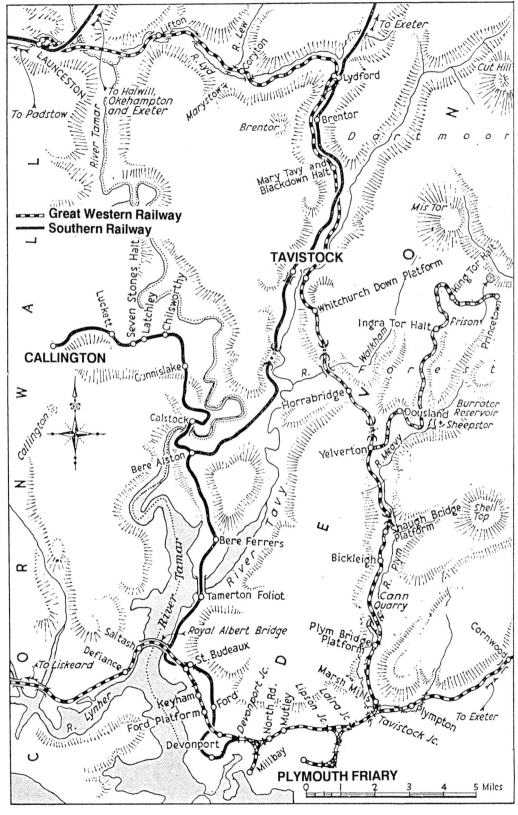

Passenger railways from 1923 to 1941 (Railway Magazine)

HISTORICAL BACKGROUND

The Great Western Railway's future main line from London reached the eastern outskirts of Plymouth when the South Devon Railway opened a temporary terminus at Laira in 1848. The line was extended to Millbay in the following year and became part of the GWR in 1878. The opening of the Cornwall Railway across the Royal Albert Bridge in 1859 completed the route through the Plymouth area, the broad gauge line being leased by the GWR in 1861 and absorbed by it in 1889.

A broad gauge branch was opened north to Tavistock via Yelverton in 1859, this being extended to Lydford and Launceston in 1865 and worked by the GWR.

The London & South Western Railway was intent on reaching Plymouth and extended its Exeter-Okehampton line to Lydford on 12th October 1874. Trains continued south on the GWR line to Plymouth, a third rail having been added for the standard gauge trains. The LSWR built their own terminus at Devonport, this opening on the same day.

Using another company's tracks was unsatisfactory and the LSWR encouraged the Plymouth, Devonport & South Western Junction Railway to build an independent route between Lydford and Plymouth. The 28 mile long line was authorised under an Act of 25th August 1883 and was opened between Devonport (former LSWR terminus) and Lydford on 2nd June 1890. The LSWR opened a new terminus at Plymouth Friary on 1st July 1891.

The Callington branch started its oper-ational life as the East Cornwall Mineral Railway, a 3ft 6ins gauge line running from a quay on the Tamar at Calstock to various mines and quarries. It was built under an Act of 9th August 1869 and was opened for goods traffic only on 7th May 1872. There was a rope worked incline at the Calstock end which precluded the carriage of passengers. The PDSWJR Act included provision for the purchase of the ECMR, its regauging and realignment prior to its connection with the main line. The work was undertaken under the 1896 Light Railways Act in 1907-08. Freight and passenger services commenced on 2nd March 1908.

The LSWR operated all trains on the PDSWJR's main line but not its branch. Both companies became part of the Southern Railway in 1923, which in turn was nationalised in 1948 to become the Southern Region of British Railways. The former SR lines west of Salisbury were transferred to the Western Region in 1963.

Complete closure of the Gunnislake- Callington section took place on 5th November 1966 and the Okehampton-Tavistock-Bere Alston route followed on 6th May 1968, except that access to Meldon Quarry was retained. The duplicated tracks south of St. Budeaux had been rationalised on 7th September 1964 by the closure of the SR route and passenger services had been withdrawn from Plymouth Friary on 15th September 1958.

All stations opened with the relevant section of line, unless otherwise stated.

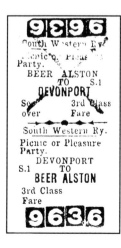

PASSENGER SERVICES

Main line

The following figures refer to Summer down trains and omit services operating on limited days each week.

A Local trains starting at Tavistock and including the one that started at either adjacent station in some years.

B Stopping trains starting at Okehampton or beyond.

C Expresses originating at Exeter or Waterloo.

	WEEKDAYS			SUNDAYS		
	A	**B**	**C**	**A**	**B**	**C**
1892	6	4	3	-	2	-
1906	6	6	4	1	3	2
1914	7	5	4	2	2	1
1924	4	6	5	1	4	1
1934	7	5	7	-	4	2
1944	7	5	3	-	4	2
1954	6	6	6	-	4	2
1963	7	7	5	-	4	3
1965	6	8	1	-	4	-
1967	1	5	-	-	2	-

A portion of the "Atlantic Coast Express" was among the expresses listed between 1934 and 1963, except in wartime. The final express shown was the through train from Brighton.

Callington Branch

The initial service comprised four trains each weekday but the SR soon improved on this and also added two trips on Sundays in April 1924.

For most of its life, the branch had six trains on weekdays and four on Sundays, the latter ceasing in 1962. Steam haulage ended in September 1964 and from the following November the service was increased to eight trains, some of which continued to Tavistock North or Exeter Central. From May 1968, all trains ran through to Plymouth. A service on Summer Sundays was reintroduced in 1990.

July 1908

BERE ALSTON and CALLINGTON ROAD (1st and 3rd class).
Plymouth, Devonport, and South Western Junction—Bere Alston and Calstock Light.

Down.	Week Days.						
	mrn	aft	b	a	mrn	aft	a
Waterloo Station, 112London ....dep.	....	....	8 50	8 50	1110	1 0	3 30
Bere Alston ....dep.	9 15	12 8	2 48	3 27	5 59	7 42	9 20
Calstock..................	9 23	1216	2 56	3 35	6 6	7 50	9 27
Gunnislake¶..............	9 35	1228	3 8	3 47	6 18	8 2	9 39
Stoke Climsland	Sig.	1241	3 21	4 1	6s31	8 15	9 49
Callington Road.......arr.	9 55	1258	3 33	4 8	6s38	8 22	9 55

Miles.	Up.	Week Days.					
		mrn	mrn	aft	aft	aft	aft
	Callington Road......dep.	7 33	10 7	1 42	5 0	6s50	8 45
1¼	Stoke Climsland ¶	7 38	Sig.	1 47	5 5	6s55	8 50
5	Gunnislake................	7 48	1022	1 57	5 15	7 10	8 55
7¾	Calstock	8 1	1034	2 8	5 27	7 22	9 7
9½	Bere Alston 112 115 arr.	8 12	1040	2 19	5 35	7 29	9 17
—	115London (Waterloo) arr	1 47	5 56	8 7	3 35	....	....

a Wednesdays only. **b** Except Wednesdays. *s* Saturdays only.
¶ "Halt" at Latchley, between Gunnislake and Stoke Climsland.

July 1914

BERE ALSTON and CALLINGTON.—Plymouth, Devonport, and South Western Junction.
Gen. Man., S. G. Hartnell, Callington.

Miles.	Down.	Week Days only.						
		mrn	mrn	mrn	mrn (Except Saturdays.)	mrn (Saturdays only.)	aft (Saturdays only.)	aft (Saturdays only.)
	Waterloo Station, 128London ....dep.	....	....	6 10	1110	1110	1 0	3 30
	131Plymouth (N. Rd.). "	7 53	1058	1 32	4 27	5 9	6 58	9 21
—	Bere Alston ....dep.	8 35	1136	2 15	5 15	5 53	7 37	10 0
1¾	Calstock..................	8 43	1144	2 23	5 22	6 0	7 45	10 8
4½	Gunnislake................	8 56	1156	2 35	5 34	6 12	7 57	1021
5½	Chilsworthy	Sig.	Sig.	Sig.	Sig.	Sig.	Sig.	Sig.
6½	Latchley	Sig.	12 3	2 41	5 40	6 18	8 4	1028
7	Seven Stones..............	Sig.	Sig.	Sig.	Sig.	Sig.	Sig.	Sig.
7¾	Luckett....................	9 9	12 8	2 47	5 46	6 23	8 8	1032
9½	Callington ‡ ....arr.	9 14	1213	2 52	5 52	6 29	8 14	1037

Miles	Up.	Week Days only.					
		mrn	mrn	aft	aft	aft	aft (Saturdays only.)
	Callington ....dep.	7 30	10 2	1 10	4 15	6 41	9 5
1¾	Luckett....................	7 36	10 7	1 15	4 20	6 46	9 10
2½	Seven Stones..............	Sig.	Sig.	Sig.	Sig.	Sig.	Sig.
3	Latchley	7 41	Sig.	1 20	4 25	6 50	Sig.
4	Chilsworthy	Sig.	Sig.	Sig.	Sig.	Sig.	Sig.
5	Gunnislake................	7 47	1017	1 25	4 32	6 56	9 20
7¾	Calstock	7 59	1029	1 37	4 44	7 8	9 32
9½	Bere Alston 128, 131 arr.	8 7	1037	1 45	4 50	7 15	9 40
20	128Plymouth(N.Rd)...arr.	8 53	1115	2 23	5 34	7 52	1019
229¾	131London (Waterloo).. "	1 47	6 a 5	8 7	3b35	....	....

NOTES.

a Arrives at 5 11 aft. on and after 20th inst.

b Via Eastleigh.

‡ Station for Stoke-climsland.

BERE ALSTON and CALLINGTON

Down — Week Days only

Miles		am	am	pm SO	am W	am	am SX	am SO	am	pm SX	pm	pm SX	pm SO	
35	London(Waterloo) dep	I‡10	..	..	..	7V28	9 0	8 35	11K0	1130	..	I 0	..	3 0	..
—	Plymouth .... dep	7 49	10 2	1220	..	I 18	2 35	2 45	4 52	5 26	6 13	..	7 18	9 26	..
—	Bere Alston .. .. dep	8 24	1040	I 0	I 58	..	3 13	3 22	5 23	6 I	7 4	7 57	10 5	..
1¼	Calstock	8 30	1046	I 8	2 4	..	3 19	3 28	5 29	6 7	7 10	8 3	1011	..
4¼	Gunnislake..	8 45	11 I	I 21	2†18	..	3 33	3 42	5 43	6†21	7 24	8†17	1025	..
5¼	Chilsworthy	8 53	11 8	I 29	..	..	3 38	3 47	5 48	..	7 33	..	1032	..
6¼	Latchley	8 58	1113	I 34	..	..	3 43	3 52	5 53	..	7 38	..	1037	..
7¼	Luckett	9 2	1117	I 39	..	..	3 48	3 57	5 57	..	7 43	..	1042	..
9¼	Callington .. .. arr	9 9	1124	I 46	..	..	3 54	4 4	6 4	..	7 50	..	1049	..

Up — Week Days only

Miles		am	am	am	am	pm	pm W	pm	pm	pm SO	
—	Callington .. .. dep	5 30	..	7 16	9 43	I 0	..	4 20	6 15	9 10	..
1¼	Luckett	5 36	..	7 22	9 49	I 6	..	4 26	6 21	9 16	..
3	Latchley	5 40	..	7 27	9 54	I 11	..	4 31	6 26	9 21	..
4	Chilsworthy	5 45	..	7 32	9 59	I 16	..	4 35	6 31	9 26	..
5	Gunnislake..	5 48	7 8	7 36	10 3	I 19	2 26	4 40	6 34	9 30	..
7¼	Calstock	6 2	7 20	7 50	1017	I 34	2 38	4 54	6 47	9 45	..
9¼	Bere Alston .. .. arr	6 10	7 29	7 59	1026	I 46	2 47	5 6	6 55	9 53	..
—	Plymouth .... arr	6 45	8 0	8 34	11u5	2Z23	3L15	5Y59	7 28	1027	..
—	London(Waterloo) arr	IS08	..	2J15	3N29	8T14	..	10 8	3a48	..	..

a am
J Arr I 50 pm on Mondays and Fridays commencing 15th July, and 2 11 pm on Saturdays.
K Dep 11 5 am on Mondays to Thursdays 29th July to 22nd August and 11 15 am on Saturdays.
L Wednesdays and Thursdays only

N Arr. 3 21 pm on Mondays to Thursdays 29th July to 22nd August and 3 53 pm on Saturdays
SO or S0 Saturdays only.
SX Mondays to Fridays.
T Arr 8 10 pm on Saturdays
u Arr 11 7 am on Saturdays.
V Saturdays only, 29th June to 17th August.

W Wednesdays, Thursdays and Saturdays only
Y Arr 6 2 pm on Saturdays
Z Arr 2 25 pm on Saturdays
† Arrival
‡ Dep 12 45 am on Saturdays

June 1963

March 1967 to May 1968.

Plymouth and Bere Alston to Gunnislake

Miles			SX		C		A SO	B				B	A SO	
—	35 PLYMOUTH .. .. .. d	05 14	07 00	..	09 30	..	13(10	13(15	..	16 38	..	18 03	..	19(25	19(30	21 35	..
—	BERE ALSTON .... d	05 40	07 29	..	10 07	..	13(45	13(50	..	17 09	..	18 34	..	19(56	20(00	22 06	..
1¾	CALSTOCK .. .. .. d	..	07 35	..	10 13	..	13(51	13(56	..	17 15	..	18 40	..	20(02	20(06	22 12	..
4½	GUNNISLAKE .... a	05 58	07 47	..	10 25	..	14(03	14(08	..	17 27	..	18 52	..	20(14	20(18	22 24	..

Gunnislake to Bere Alston and Plymouth

Miles			C SX	C			B		A SO						
—	GUNNISLAKE .... d	06 05	07 51	..	..	10 40	14(30	..	14(35	17 32	..	18 56	..	20 25	..	22 30	..
2¼	CALSTOCK .. .. d	06 17	08 03	..	..	10 52	14(42	..	14(47	17 44	..	19 08	..	20 37	..	22 42	..
4½	BERE ALSTON .... a	06 24	08 10	..	..	10 59	14(49	..	14(54	17 51	..	19 15	..	20 44	..	22 49	..
—	35 PLYMOUTH .. .. a	06 56	08 37	..	..	11e34	15(23	..	15(25	18 24	..	19 45	..	21 15	..	23 16	..

A 27 May to 16 September
B Not on Saturdays 27 May to 16 September
C From or to Exeter (Table 35)

b On Saturdays arr 11 47
c Sunday mornings
e On Saturdays 27 May to 16 September arr 11 31

TAVISTOCK NORTH

1.   The station was situated high above the town centre on the west side of the Tavy Valley and was at the north end (left) of the viaduct. Access to the down platform was through the left arch; the road adjacent to the embankment led to the up side. (Lens of Sutton)

The 1906 map shows the goods yard, the size of which was restricted by the topography.

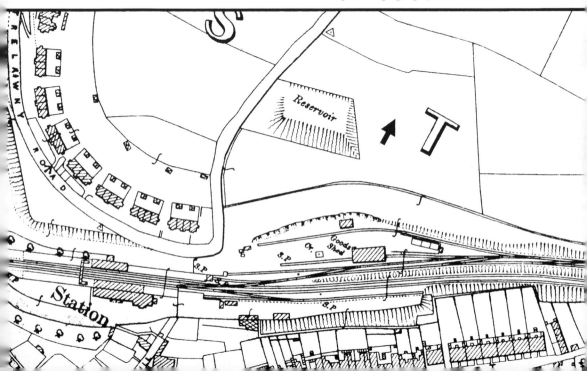

2. Passengers wait for an up train in 1937. Space restrictions meant that the larger building was on the down side but generous canopies were provided on both platforms. (H.C.Casserley coll.)

3. The Plymouth to Brighton train was usually the longest on the route. It is crossing the viaduct behind class U1 2-6-0 no. 1892 on 13th May 1939. The crossover was used by terminating trains on local services from Plymouth Friary. (J.R.W.Kirkby)

4. Three dormers with ornamental ridge tiles and finials gave character to the south elevation on the down side. Bold brick quoins are other notable features in this 1950 view. After closure, the building became a residence and was named "Beeching's Folly". (H.C.Casserley coll.)

5. The station received the suffix "North" on 26th September 1949 and goods traffic continued until 28th February 1966. The goods yard at Tavistock South (ex-GWR) on the other side of the valley closed in 1964. On the right is the down berthing siding. The signal box remained in use until the withdrawal of passenger services in 1968. (Lens of Sutton)

6.   Very severe weather conditions on 29th December 1962 necessitated a rescue train, hauled by no. 34063 *229 Squadron*. Three engines had become snowed up in Sawton Cutting, north of Bridestowe, but this train was unable to proceed beyond Tavistock. It returned with its gang of men to Devonport Kings Road at 1.02pm, running wrong road as far as Bere Alston. (M.Dart)

Other views of this station and of problems with snow drifts can be seen in the companion album *Exeter to Tavistock*.

BERE ALSTON

7. A PDSWJR brake van stands in the yard while an oil-lit four-wheeled coach, with bulbous duckets for the guard, waits at the end of a train at the branch platform. The spelling was Beer Alston until November 1897. (R.M.Casserley coll.)

The 1906 map has an embankment on the left ready for the new line to Calstock. There is also space for it between the goods yard and the up platform.

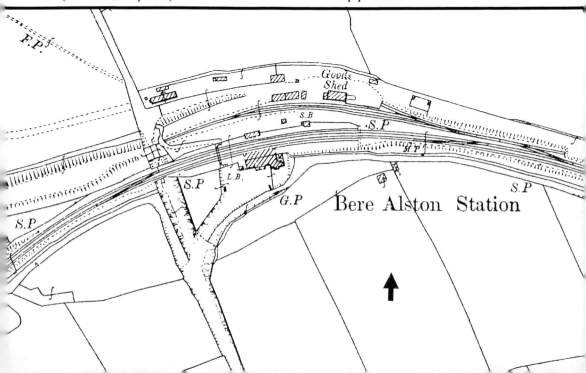

8. The landform hereabouts meant that there was no straight length of track on which to build a station close to the village, which is south of the line. This eastward view includes the original wooden footbridge. (R.M.Casserley coll.)

9. The ECMR had two Neilson 0-4-0Ts which were regauged and converted to 0-4-2Ts. They were sold in 1909 and 1912, no. 2 receiving the name *Hesperus* and appearing in several photographs that can be seen in our *Branch Line to Selsey*. Here is one of the two standard Hawthorn Leslie 0-6-2Ts purchased by the PDSWJR in 1907. It was given the number E758 by the SR in 1923, being named *Lord St Levan* originally and listed as no. 5. (R.M.Casserley coll.)

10. The 3.0pm from Waterloo arrives behind class N 2-6-0 no. A837 of 1924 on 14th June 1926, while another tender engine stands at the branch platform. The goods shed is also evident in this view from the footbridge. (H.C.Casserley)

11. Two westward views from the footbridge follow. The Callington branch is near the signals on the left of this picture from 23rd May 1935. Class O2 0-4-4T no. 203 is on the bridge over the road to a farm. (H.C.Casserley)

12. Class U1 2-6-0 no. 1890 is waiting to leave with the 8.46am Exeter Central to Plymouth Friary on 13th May 1939. Visible above the boiler is the 15mph speed restriction sign for the branch. (J.R.W.Kirkby)

13. Seen in 1947 is one of the unusual coaches fitted with gates and used on local Southern services in the Plymouth area. Milk was often carried on passenger trains. (S.C.Nash)

14. No. 6557 is an example of the brake version of the "Plymouth Gate" stock and was recorded in June 1949. The nearest compartment is for first class ticket holders. (J.H.Aston)

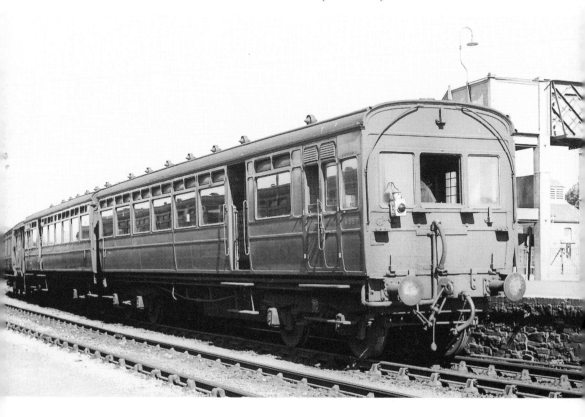

BERE ALSTON	1928	1936
No. of passenger tickets issued	32413	37889
No. of season tickets issued	192	455
No. of passenger tickets collected	50793	50671
No. of telegrams	8911	5254
No. of parcels forwarded	3665	4991
No. of parcels received	2045	3153
Horses forwarded	7	3
Milk forwarded - Cans 1928/Gallons 1936	4060	2619
Milk received - Cans 1928/Gallons 1936	356	132
General goods forwarded (tons)	218	289
General goods received (tons)	1416	1849
Coal, coke etc. received (tons)	1311	1783
Other minerals forwarded (tons)	204	-
Other minerals received (tons)	498	285
Trucks livestock forwarded	36	40
Trucks livestock received	17	-
Lavatory pennies	420	500

15. The 6.55pm stopping train from Tavistock North to Plymouth Friary waits to leave behind class M7 no. 30375 on 21st June 1950. The wooden footbridge was replaced by this concrete and steel hybrid. (J.J.Smith)

16.   The sidings visible in pictures 11 and 12 were level, as normal. The branch dropped at 1 in 40 and was soon at a lower level. Class O2 no. 30183 leaves with the 5.23pm to Callington on 21st September 1955. The pump and tanks were part of the push-pull equipment. (S.C.Nash)

17.   The LMS designed 2-6-2Ts were introduced to the area in 1952. No. 41316 is accelerating the 6.55pm from Tavistock North over the crossover on 1st June 1959. The ex-SR coaches are of Bulleid's design. (S.C.Nash)

18.   The branch signals were of contrasting styles. Upper quadrant on two old running rails and lower quadrant on a tapered wooden post of some antiquity. The branch had its own signal box (near the footbridge) until 13th February 1927. (S.C.Nash)

←

19. A DMU stands in the goods yard on 18th February 1966. Freight traffic ceased ten days later but the three sidings remained until the end of 1968. The unusual shelter does not appear in picture no. 10, but building work was in progress when it was taken. (Wessex coll.)

P. D. & S W. Jct. Rly
This Ticket is issued subject to the By-laws Regulations & Conditions stated in the Company's Time Tables Bills & Notices
CALLINGTON
(For Stoke Climsland) to
Crediton
Via Bere Alston &
3rd CLASS Actual Fare 6/8

←

20. The south elevation was similar in style to that at Tavistock North. The toilet block had lost the massive ventilator featured in picture no. 8 but retained a Royal Mail letterbox. (Wessex coll.)

21. The 12.20 from Gunnislake had passed behind the signal box to reach the down main line on 16th July 1969. Major rationalisation took place on 7th September 1970 when the line to St.Budeaux was singled, the 30-lever signal box was closed and the track simplified, as shown in the next picture. (G.Gillham)

22. DMU no. 954 forms the 12.00 from Plymouth on 18th July 1990. On the right is the 1970 connection to the branch to Gunnislake. One rod moves the point blades and the other operates their locking bar. (D.Mitchell)

23. Having changed the points the driver returns to his train on 18th September 1996. In his hand is the train staff, the pointed part of which forms the key to unlock the ground frame seen in the previous picture. Two train conductors were required on this busy train, the 07.40 from Gunnislake. (V.Mitchell)

Callington Branch

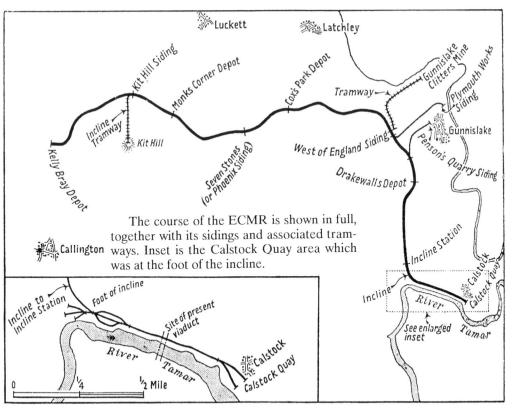

The course of the ECMR is shown in full, together with its sidings and associated tramways. Inset is the Calstock Quay area which was at the foot of the incline.

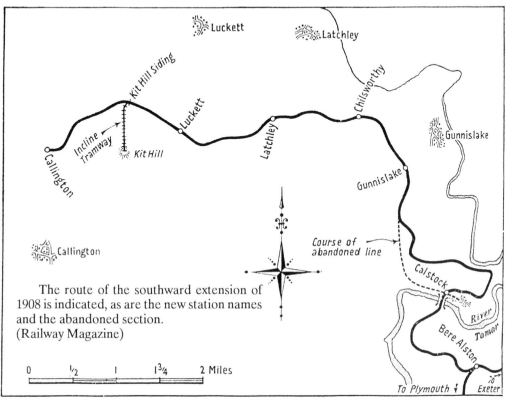

The route of the southward extension of 1908 is indicated, as are the new station names and the abandoned section.
(Railway Magazine)

CALSTOCK VIADUCT

24. The major engineering requirement in the scheme to upgrade the ECMR was the construction of a 120 ft high viaduct over the River Tamar. The engineer for the conversion, but not the viaduct, was H.F.Stephens, now better known as Colonel Stephens the specialist in the construction and management of light railways throughout England and Wales. The one-ton concrete blocks were cast on the site, all the new works being undertaken by Galbraith & Church although often attributed to Stephens. (J.Chilman coll.)

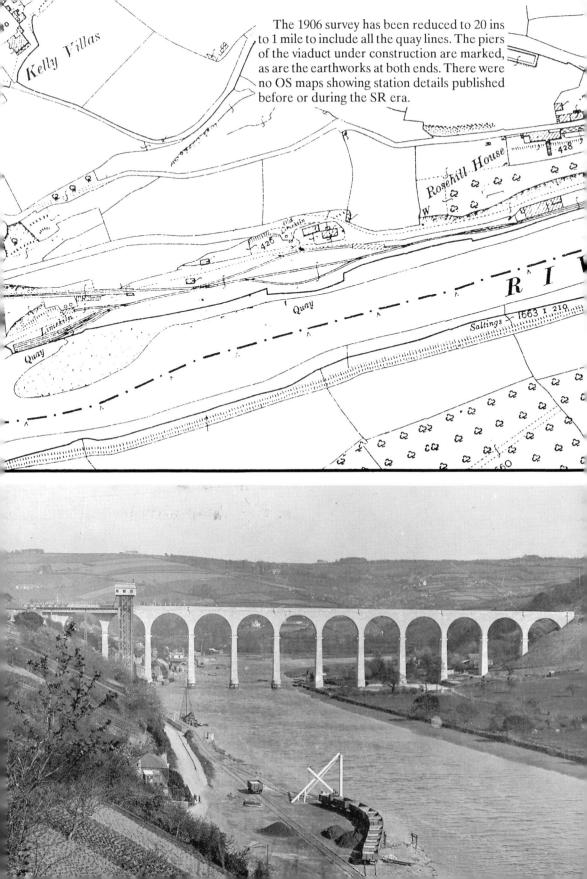

The 1906 survey has been reduced to 20 ins to 1 mile to include all the quay lines. The piers of the viaduct under construction are marked, as are the earthworks at both ends. There were no OS maps showing station details published before or during the SR era.

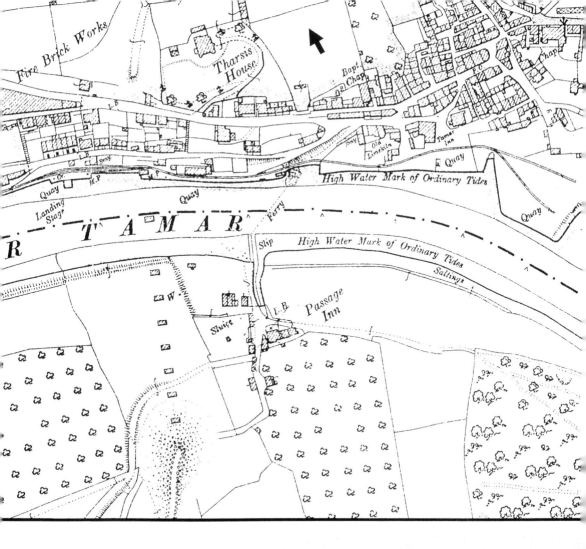

25.   A northward view includes some of the
lines on Calstock Quay. They were all converted to standard gauge but the incline was
closed in favour of a wagon hoist, left.
(M.Dart coll.)

26.   The wagon hoist was steam operated and
had a 20-ton weight limit, so only one wagon
was moved at a time over the 112 ft difference
in height. It was little used, owing to the decline
in the local extractive industries, and was sold
and dismantled in 1934. (E.W.Fry coll.)

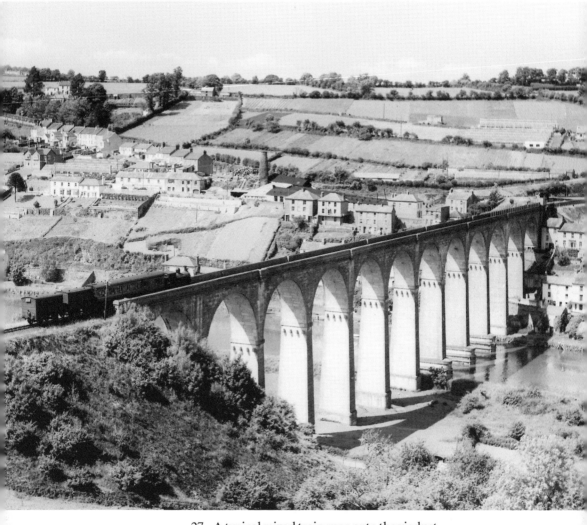

27. A typical mixed train runs onto the viaduct on 3rd June 1959. It is the 3.15pm from Bere Alston to Callington and is headed by class O2 0-4-4T no. 30225. (S.C.Nash)

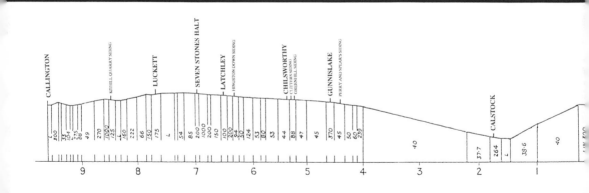

CALSTOCK

28.   The incline between the quays and main line of the ECMR was on a gradient of 1 in 6 and was provided with a steam powered wind-ing drum. Shunting on the quay lines was undertaken by this horse. (Unknown)

29.   The *SS Albion* is moored at one of the four quays of the ECMR, sometime before the viaduct was built. A pleasure steamer is included in this picture as well as in no. 24. There is also a small structure of interest to students of sanitation. (M.Dart coll.)

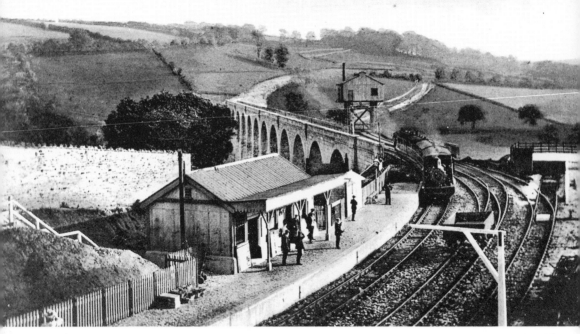

CALSTOCK	1928	1936
No. of passenger tickets issued	11991	12416
No. of season tickets issued	59	76
No. of passenger tickets collected	13615	14439
No. of telegrams	-	349
No. of parcels forwarded	6124	16722
No. of parcels received	1395	1904
Horses forwarded	4	-
Milk forwarded - Cans 1928/Gallons 1936	2	20200
Milk received - Cans 1928/Gallons 1936	2	10
General goods forwarded (tons)	125	95
General goods received (tons)	318	258
Coal, coke etc. received (tons)	498	914
Other minerals forwarded (tons)	-	-
Other minerals received (tons)	97	33
Trucks livestock forwarded	2	-
Trucks livestock received	-	-
Lavatory pennies	240	90

30. A postcard view reveals the relationship of the viaduct to the station, the building of which is similar to those found on other lines engineered by Colonel Stephens. The sidings to the cattle dock and wagon hoist are also evident. (Lens of Sutton)

2nd - SINGLE	SINGLE - 2nd
3296	Ford (Devon) to
Ford (Devon) Gunnislake	Ford (Devon) Gunnislake
GUNNISLAKE	3296
via Bere Alston	
(S) 2/11 Fare 2/11 (S)	
For conditions see over	conditions see over

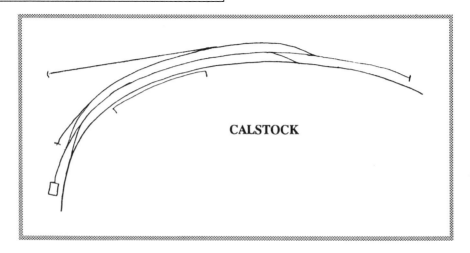

CALSTOCK

31. From left to right in this 1966 panorama is the ten-lever signal box, the water tower, the 1908 corrugated-iron clad building, the gents (seldom provided by Stephens), the lamp room and the coal shed. (Wessex coll.)

32. The original four-lever frame was replaced by one with ten in 1937, three of which were spare. The box closed on 5th May 1968. This March 1966 view includes vans on one of the two goods loops. Up to 14 vans of strawberries were despatched daily in peak season. The building on the right housed a ground frame until 1937. (Wessex coll.)

33. Goods traffic ceased on 28th February 1966 but some van bodies remained and one was photographed on 29th March 1982. By that time a new shelter had arrived. (J.Scrace)

BETWEEN BERE ALSTON AND CALLINGTON.

Loads of trains, etc.—The maximum loads of passenger trains between Bere Alston and Callington and vice versa are as follows :—

Nos. of engine.	Maximum load.
3125, 3298, 3314, 3329, 3520, 735, 756.	3 bogie vehicles (non-corridor).
177–179 inc., 181–183 inc., 185, 187, 191–201 inc., 203, 204, 207, 212–214 inc., 216–218 inc., 221–225 inc., 227–236 inc., 557, 563, 565, 567, 571, 574, 576–578 inc., 580, 584, 586, 587, 590, 592, 657–666 inc.	4 bogie vehicles (non-corridor). 4 bogie vehicles (non-corridor) and one P.L. van under favourable weather and rail conditions.
3029, 3083, 3101, 3153, 3154, 3155, 3163, 3167, 3397, 3400, 3433, 3436, 3439–3442 inc., 3496, 3506, 3509, 3515, 757, 758.	5 bogie vehicles (non-corridor). 6 bogie vehicles (non-corridor) under favourable weather and rail conditions.

A heavy goods brake van fitted with sanding apparatus must be provided at the rear of all goods trains run on the Bere Alston and Callington line.

GUNNISLAKE

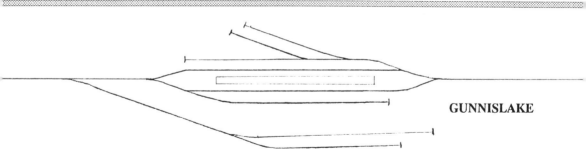

GUNNISLAKE

GUNNISLAKE	1928	1936
No. of passenger tickets issued	19183	23397
No. of season tickets issued	36	79
No. of passenger tickets collected	28520	30719
No. of telegrams	-	-
No. of parcels forwarded	3870	7420
No. of parcels received	3141	4666
Horses forwarded	-	2
Milk forwarded - Cans 1928/Gallons 1936	9423	31694
Milk received - Cans 1928/Gallons 1936	1	17
General goods forwarded (tons)	204	80
General goods received (tons)	1942	1445
Coal, coke etc. received (tons)	2910	2413
Other minerals forwarded (tons)	140	27
Other minerals received (tons)	182	144
Trucks livestock forwarded	1	6
Trucks livestock received	-	-
Lavatory pennies	240	688

34. Built on the site of Drakewalls Depot, the station was the only passing point on the line and had an island platform. On the up side is Hawthorn Leslie 0-6-0T no. 3 *A.S.Harris*, the third new locomotive purchased by Stephens for the PDSWJR and named after one of its directors. Like the two 0-6-2Ts, it was built in 1907. It was renumbered 756 by the SR in 1923 and worked in this area until 1931. It was scrapped in 1951 and is seen better in picture no. 112. (Lens of Sutton)

35.   This photograph from 22nd June 1950 includes (right) ex-PDSWJR 0-6-2T *Earl of Mount Edgcumbe*, which was named after another director. On the left is the other 0-6-2T from 1907, *Lord St.Levan*. These powerful machines weighed almost 50 tons each and were permitted to haul six non-corridor bogie coaches on the branch on dry rails. They were PDSWJR nos. 4 and 5, the SR applying the numbers 757 and 758. The vehicle crossing on the right allowed parcels and milk churns to be conveyed with ease. (J.J.Smith)

GUNNISLAKE.

When, in connection with the marshalling of an up goods train, it is necessary for vehicles to be shunted from the goods yard to the up loop line, this must only be done by the engine, and after the vehicles have been brought to a stand on the up loop line a sufficient number of wagon brakes must, before the engine is detached, be firmly applied at the Calstock end to prevent the vehicles moving.

After the marshalling of the train has been completed and a tablet for the Calstock section withdrawn, the engine may be permitted to proceed over the down loop, under the control of the person in charge of the shunting operations, for the purpose of being attached to the front of the train standing in the up loop. The person in charge of the shunting operations must satisfy himself that the points are in proper position for the movements required to be made.

Sandhill Park siding.—The gradient of the siding rises 1 in 35 from the catch points near the entrance for a distance of about 85 yards, at which point a second catch tongue is provided operated by a hand lever, and this catch tongue must be held for movements thereover in the facing direction.   Beyond this point the gradient is gradually reduced for a distance of about 17 yards, and is on the level thence to the stop blocks.

Wagons for the siding must be drawn from Gunnislake station with a brake van at the rear in which the Guard must ride.   On arrival at the siding the brake of the van must be firmly applied and a sufficient number of wagon brakes securely applied, after which the engine must be uncoupled and proceed to the siding to draw out the outgoing wagons. The latter must then be coupled to the ingoing wagons, and the whole of the wagons propelled into the siding.

36.   A panorama from 21st September 1955 includes class O2 no. 30183 with the 3.15pm Bere Alston to Callington mixed train. Loaded stone wagons await despatch on the left; on the right is the goods yard which was in use until 28th February 1966. (S.C.Nash)

37.   A troop of trucks awaits the next crop of soft fruit. Here we look towards Callington in June 1965, the passenger exit being on the right. The two crossings evident in the previous picture have been reduced to one. (R.M.Casserley)

38. The way out was down a steep slope and through a subway under the down line. The A390 passed under the line in the distance near the signal. This is a 1966 photograph. A jam factory opened nearby in October 1935, greatly increasing the parcel traffic. (Wessex coll.)

39. The signal box was at the end of the up siding and it had ten levers, all in use, but the single line instruments were in the office on the platform. The box was situated beyond the left borders of pictures 35 and 36 and was closed on 5th May 1968. (Wessex coll.)

40. The former cattle dock can be seen on the right of this photograph of the 12.20 to Plymouth on 16th July 1969. The line to Callington had been closed in November 1966 and lifted in June 1967. For two years, trains arrived on the right and departed from the left platform. (G.Gillham)

41. A simple shelter punctuated the desolate scene when photographers arrived on 5th December 1981. At least passengers could travel direct to Plymouth without having to change at Bere Alston. (C.L.Caddy)

42. The subway had been infilled and the site of the down line and goods yard had become a car park by the time that no. 150242 was photo- graphed on 2nd October 1993. (E.Wilmshurst)

43. The bridge over the main road was removed, the original station site having been abandoned on 21st January 1994. This new platform was opened on 6th June 1994 at a much lower level. Here is the 10.20 departure on 18th March 1995. (V.Mitchell)

PLYMOUTH, DEVONPORT AND SOUTH WESTERN JUNCTION RAILWAY.

(Bere Alston and Callington Line.)

CHEAP

MARKET TICKETS

TO

Plymouth & Devonport

WILL BE ISSUED

THURSDAYS & SATURDAYS,

AS UNDER :—

	A.M.	A.M.	FARES:
			3rd Class Return from any Station TO
Callington Road	7.23	9.50	
Stoke Climsland	7.32	9.57	Devonport **1/8**
Latchley - - -	7.39	10.3	Plymouth **1/10** (North Rd.)
Gunnislake - -	7.51	10.13	
Calstock - - -	8.8	10.28	Plymouth **2/-** (Friary)

Available for return by any Train on the day of issue only.

Children under Three Years of Age, Free; Three and under Twelve, Half-fares.

The Tickets are not transferable, and are subject to the conditions published in the Company's Time Tables and Bills, and in the General Notice containing the conditions on which Tickets are issued to Passengers. Attention is particularly directed to the conditions limiting the availability of Cheap Tickets.

Passengers travelling without personal luggage with these Cheap Market Tickets may carry with them 60 lbs. of marketing goods free of charge (at their own risk), all excess over that weight will be charged for.

February, 1908.   (*By order*) **J. W. BURCHELL,** *Secretary.*

BRADBURY, AGNEW, & CO. LD., PRINTERS, LONDON AND TONBRIDGE.   (4211-2-08.)

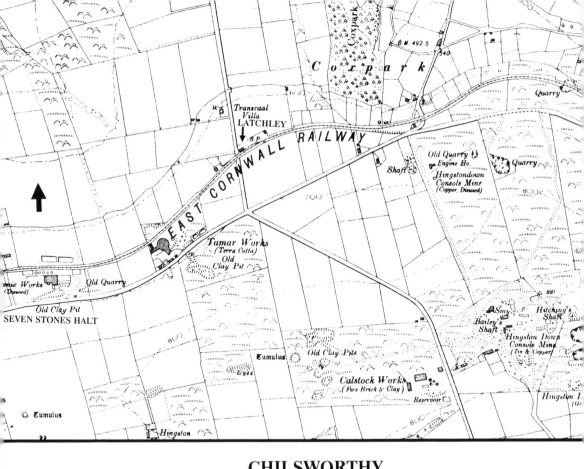

CHILSWORTHY

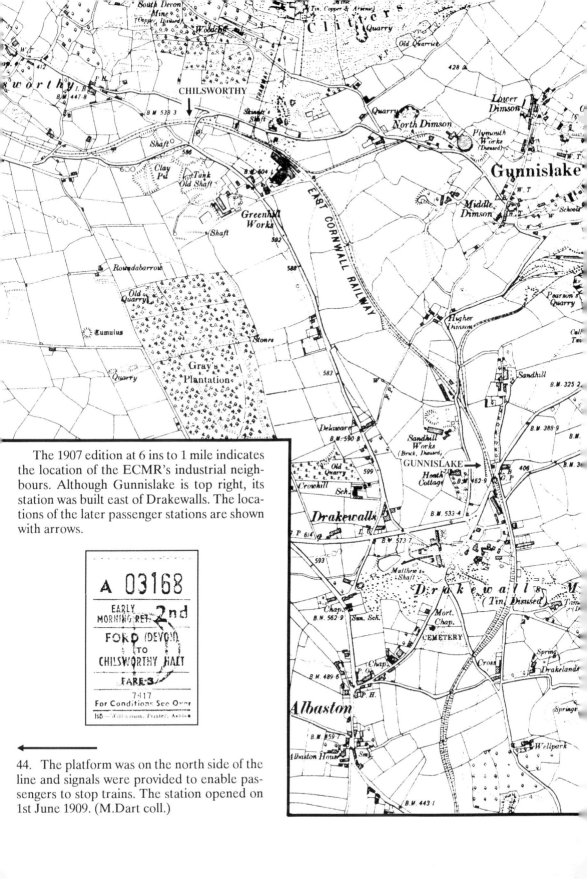

CHILSWORTHY

EAST CORNWALL RAILWAY

GUNNISLAKE →

The 1907 edition at 6 ins to 1 mile indicates the location of the ECMR's industrial neighbours. Although Gunnislake is top right, its station was built east of Drakewalls. The locations of the later passenger stations are shown with arrows.

A 03168

EARLY
MORNING RET. 2nd

FORD (DEVON)
TO
CHILSWORTHY HALT

FARE 3/-

7417
For Conditions See Over

H3—Williamson, Printer, Ashton

←

44. The platform was on the north side of the line and signals were provided to enable passengers to stop trains. The station opened on 1st June 1909. (M.Dart coll.)

45. A two-lever ground frame was provided in 1928 at the siding of Hill, Westlake & Company, brick and tile manufacturers. Their premises were requisitioned by the Ministry of Food in 1942 and the siding was removed in 1959. (R.M.Casserley coll.)

46. There are signs of mineral extraction beyond the train which was hauled by class O2 no. 30192 on 27th June 1956. It is the 1.0pm from Callington. The scenery for tourists is on the right. The platform edge and sign posts were still visible 40 years later. (J.H.Aston)

47. East of the station was the site of Clitters siding, which was in use until 1928. Further east, but on the south side, was Cocking's Sand Hill Park sidings, which were usable until January 1961. Westwards were Whiterock sidings (1925-62) and Hingston Down siding, a loop leading to a quarry railway. Both were south of the line. (Wessex coll.)

LUCKETT.

Whiterocks (Hingston Down Quarries Co.) siding.—The siding rises 1 in 40 from a point near the boundary gate for a distance of 450 yards from the main line and terminates in a shunting neck which extends 100 yards beyond the trailing points connecting with the extended sidings.

There are two sidings serving the Quarry Company's plant, which extend from the shunting neck in a westerly direction on a rising gradient for a distance of 360 yards. These two sidings are provided with two crossover roads, the second or westernmost being for the passage of wagons only.

Under no circumstances must the Company's engine pass beyond, or over, the second of the two crossover roads.

The Porter in charge at Luckett will assist with the working of the train calling at the siding.

The train must be brought to a stand with the engine well clear of the siding points to enable the required number of wagons to be attached without having to set the train back before re-starting.

Before detaching the engine or wagons from the train, the Guard must take care to pin down a sufficient number of wagon brakes on the portion of the train left standing on the running line, and also see that the brake in the van is securely applied, after which the engine and wagons which have been detached will be taken to the shunting neck situated on the higher level where the necessary shunting work will be carried out.

Before a movement is made from the shunting neck down the incline to the main line, the catch tongue at the head and the points of the catch road at the foot of the incline, which are normally open, must be held over.

On completion of the work at the extended sidings, the Guard must be careful to pin down a sufficient number of wagon brakes before proceeding to propel the wagons towards the running line. Great care must be exercised in the manipulation of the trap points in the sidings.

The Porter in charge at Luckett station must remain in charge of the rear part of the train left on the running line and hold the trap road points in position for the engine and wagons to pass over to the train ; after the engine and wagons have been coupled to the train standing on the running line, he must close and lock the gate, replace the points to their normal position, withdraw the tablet and hand it to the Driver, accompany the train to Gunnislake station, and return thence to Luckett by the next train.

During the whole of the time the work of the siding is being performed, the points in the running line must remain set for the siding.

LATCHLEY

48.   The buildings were those of the ECMR which explains the low doorway of the goods shed. The siding disappears behind the goods platform which shows more clearly in the next picture. The house survives as a dwelling and was photographed in about 1950. (M.Dart coll.)

49.   The 10.50am from Bere Alston was recorded on 28th June 1956. The train is climbing at 1 in 100 and so the siding finished at a lower level to avoid wagons being left on a gradient. (J.H.Aston)

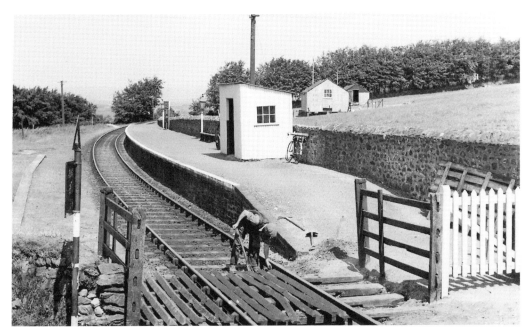

50. Seldom photographed were the men who toiled, usually out of sight, to maintain a safe and tidy railway. The siding has gone; in its final years it was only used for full wagon loads. (J.H.Aston)

SEVEN STONES HALT

51. The halt was opened on 15th June 1910 to serve the Phoenix Pleasure Ground. This was created on the site of the Phoenix Brickworks and was a popular destination for Sunday School outings. It closed in September 1917 owing to wartime restrictions. This is a view eastward in about 1950; the gradient post shows the transition from 1 in 85 to 1 in 200. (R.M.Casserley coll.)

LUCKETT

52.   The 4.23pm from Callington waits while the porter loads some strawberries on 27th June 1956. The land beyond the canopy ac-commodated a carriage shed, built in 1910 and used for hay drying during World War I. The house was still in use in 1995. (J.H.Aston)

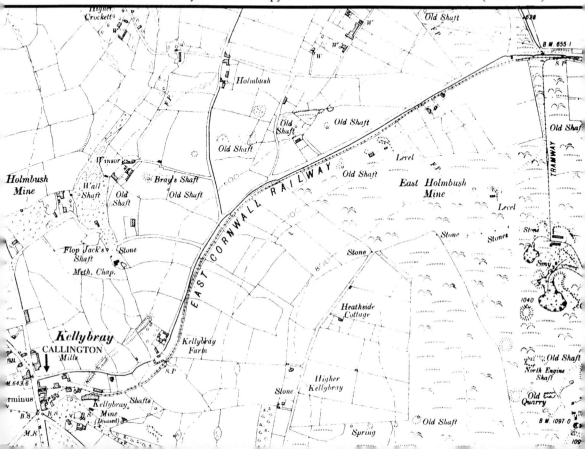

53. The goods loop was on the ground on the right until 1962. Similar building style can be seen in *Branch Line to Tenterden* and other Middleton Press albums featuring the Stephens empire. The station was named Stoke Climsland until 1st November 1909. (Wessex coll.)

The right edge of this map continues from the left part of the previous one. The direction of access to the Kithill Tramway was reversed during the conversion to standard gauge. The terminus at Kellybray (left) became Callington Road at that time. It was renamed Callington on 1st November 1909. The population of Callington, one mile to the south, was 1888 in 1891 and 2212 in 1951.

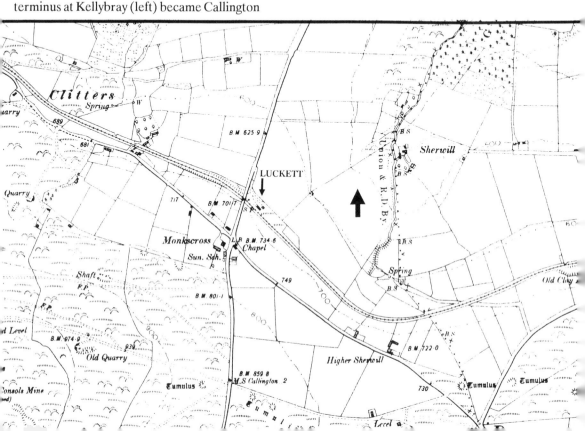

LUCKETT	1928	1936
No. of passenger tickets issued	3695	3573
No. of season tickets issued	6	-
No. of passenger tickets collected	3368	1882
No. of telegrams	-	15
No. of parcels forwarded	115	150
No. of parcels received	126	158
Horses forwarded	-	-
Milk forwarded - Cans 1928/Gallons 1936	2639	50327
Milk received - Cans 1928/Gallons 1936	2	26
General goods forwarded (tons)	19	28
General goods received (tons)	295	283
Coal, coke etc. received (tons)	701	1315
Other minerals forwarded (tons)	26374	1132
Other minerals received (tons)	91	423
Trucks livestock forwarded	-	-
Trucks livestock received	-	-
Lavatory pennies	-	-

54. Over one mile west of Luckett, the Kit Hill siding branched off on the south side to link with the line to Griffiths' Quarry - see last map. The siding was taken out of use in December 1954. (R.M.Casserley coll.)

```
2nd · SINGLE        SINGLE · 2nd

0805        Ford (Devon) to        0805
        Ford (Devon)          Ford (Devon)

        Callington            Callington
0805        CALLINGTON        0805
            Via Bere Alston
        (S)    3/2   FARE   3/2   (S)
     For condit'ns see over  For condit'ns see over
```

Kit Hill (Wm. Griffiths & Co.) siding.—The shunting operations are performed by the Guards of the trains concerned.

Wagons for the siding are conveyed from Callington and must be attached next the engine of up goods trains. On arrival of the train at the siding, the van brake must be fully applied and a sufficient number of wagon brakes securely applied, after which the wagons to be placed in the siding must be uncoupled and the hand brakes applied. The engine must then be detached and run forward beyond the points leading to the siding, the points set for the siding, and the wagons allowed to gravitate into the siding clear of the catch points. The points must then be set for the running line, and the engine recoupled to the train.

Traffic from the siding will be taken on by down goods trains and conveyed to Callington en route to destination, the van brakes to be applied and a sufficient number of wagon brakes securely applied before the engine is detached from the train and allowed to proceed into the siding for the wagons.

CALLINGTON

55. The PDSWJR did not apply its initials (or numbers) to its locomotives but its wagons had an abbreviated form. No ownership indication can be seen in photographs of their coaches. *Earl of Mount Edgcumbe* is on the left and *Lord St.Levan* on the right. (Lens of Sutton)

56. This and the previous picture show the engine shed when its entrance was at the west end. It was at the other end from May 1928, when the platform was lengthened by 30 yds. This ground frame was moved 20 yds nearer to the shed at that time and designated "B". The eastern one ("A") was new at that time. (Lens of Sutton)

CALLINGTON	1928	1936
No. of passenger tickets issued	20349	23384
No. of season tickets issued	4	12
No. of passenger tickets collected	27095	32769
No. of telegrams	-	370
No. of parcels forwarded	1627	2738
No. of parcels received	3104	4777
Horses forwarded	26	4
Milk forwarded - Cans 1928/Gallons 1936	698	4742
Milk received - Cans 1928/Gallons 1936	4	1
General goods forwarded (tons)	1177	403
General goods received (tons)	8187	10871
Coal, coke etc. received (tons)	3179	3387
Other minerals forwarded (tons)	1874	1942
Other minerals received (tons)	2489	1843
Trucks livestock forwarded	186	365
Trucks livestock received	6	4
Lavatory pennies	672	816

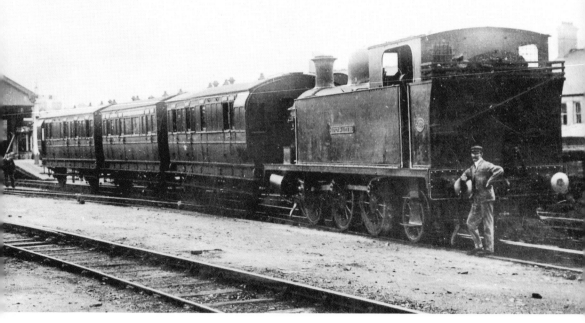

57. The PDSWJR optimistically purchased 16 secondhand coaches from the LSWR and North London Railway in 1908, all four-wheelers of this type. Six were sold in 1911 and four LSWR bogies were bought in 1921. The locomotive is *Lord St.Levan*. (R.M.Casserley coll.)

58. The station housed the offices of the PDSWJR until 1923. H.F.Stephens was appointed the line's first manager agreeing to attend to its affairs on two days each week. This he failed to do and so he was dismissed on 30th June 1910. He assumed the rank of Lieutenant Colonel during World War I. (Lens of Sutton)

59.   The SR replaced *A.S.Harris* by various members of the O2 class and ex-LSWR bogie stock became the norm for years. This photograph is probably from the 1930s when the concrete fencing is likely to have been provided by the SR. (R.M.Casserley coll.)

60.   The revised position of the ground frame in relation to the engine shed is evident in this picture from 18th August 1954. After arrival, class O2 no. 30225 propelled its train back to the loop and has now run forward before reversing to run round. The starting signal was the last to survive from the PDSWJR. (H.C.Casserley)

61.   One of the original 0-6-2Ts plus one O2 was the usual allocation from Friary Shed for over 40 years. The former were replaced by LMR class 2s in 1952, being used, like their predecessors, mainly on turns involving freight or mixed trains. Nos 41306 and 30192 were recorded on 27th June 1956. (J.H.Aston)

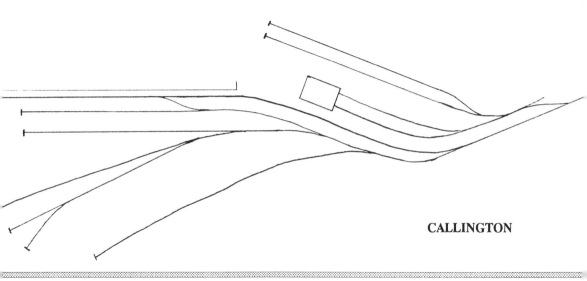

62. The east end of the shed and the water column were photographed on 17th June 1962. Steam working ceased at the end of September 1964. Diesel locomotives worked freight services thereafter but passengers were conveyed in DMUs. (J.M.Tolson/F.Hornby)

63. The overall roof is thought to predate the gauge conversion, and that the iron-clad offices seen in picture no. 58 were added by Stephens. The lean-to evident in picture 59 had gone by the 1950s. The goods shed is in the background; a 3-ton capacity crane was available therein and there was another in the yard. (Wessex coll.)

64. A second view from March 1966 includes the 80ft high chimney of Kit Hill Great Consols tin mine. There was a goods shed and extensive accommodation for animal feedstuffs. The 1916 cattle dock can be seen between the two buildings. Freight and passenger services were both withdrawn on 5th November 1966. The land now forms the Beeching Way Industrial Park. (Wessex coll.)

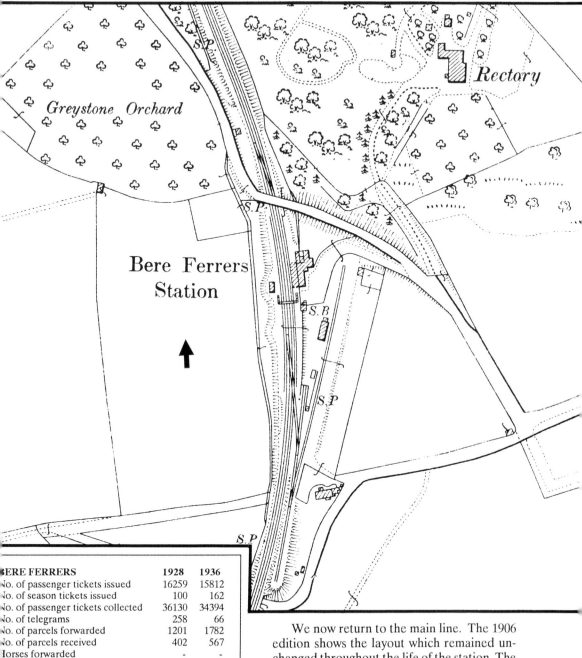

Rectory

Greystone Orchard

Bere Ferrers
Station

S.P

S.B

S.P

S.P

BERE FERRERS	1928	1936
No. of passenger tickets issued	16259	15812
No. of season tickets issued	100	162
No. of passenger tickets collected	36130	34394
No. of telegrams	258	66
No. of parcels forwarded	1201	1782
No. of parcels received	402	567
Horses forwarded	-	-
Milk forwarded - Cans 1928/Gallons 1936	2963	15552
Milk received - Cans 1928/Gallons 1936	2	-
General goods forwarded (tons)	140	44
General goods received (tons)	181	92
Coal, coke etc. received (tons)	89	80
Other minerals forwarded (tons)	65	-
Other minerals received (tons)	113	-
Trucks livestock forwarded	49	11
Trucks livestock received	3	-
Lavatory pennies	300	167

We now return to the main line. The 1906 edition shows the layout which remained unchanged throughout the life of the station. The village is east of the station but its population changed little from 1891 to 1961, being a little under 2000 in that period.

65. A southward view includes the goods shed (above the canopy) and the connection to the goods yard. Freight traffic ceased on 8th Oc- tober 1962 but the sidings were not taken out of use until June 1965. (Lens of Sutton)

66. A photograph of the eastern elevation includes the signal box, which was in use until 27th October 1968. The two crossovers had been eliminated earlier. (Lens of Sutton)

67. The station buildings and goods yard were sold and a private collection of railway relics was established on the site. Seen in 1993, this Hunslet 0-4-0 diesel had previously worked at the Ernesettle Naval Depot, three miles to the south. (P.G.Barnes)

68. Owing to a ban on main line locomotives on the branch, "The Pixie Returns" railtour on 23rd October 1994 to Bere Alston had a class 08 diesel shunter at each end. This is no. 08663. The signal box had recently been moved from Pinhoe and displays the spelling used until 18th November 1897. (D.Mitchell)

69. The main engineering feature on the main line is the Tavy Viaduct with its mixture of bowstring girders and masonry arches. No. 34069 *Hawkinge* is running tender first with the 6.48pm Tavistock North to Plymouth on 9th May 1961. (S.C.Nash)

0090

SOUTHERN RAILWAY.
Issued subject to the Bye-laws,
Regulations & Conditions in the
Company's Bills and Notices.

Monthly advertised
St. Budeaux to
TAMERTON FOLIOT
Third Class Fare 7½d
NOT TRANSFERABLE.

SOUTHERN RAILWAY.
MONTHLY RETURN

Tamerton F.
St. Budeaux

Tamerton Foliot to
ST. BUDEAUX
Third Class. Fare 7½d
The Passenger is requested to
see this ticket punched at the
time of issue

0090

0544

SOUTHERN RAILWAY.
Issued subject to the Bye-laws,
Regulations & Conditions in the
Company's Bills and Notices.

H.M.F. on LEAVE.
Tavistock to
TAMERTON FOLIOT
Third Class. Fare 1/10
NOT TRANSFERABLE.

SOUTHERN RAILWAY.
H.M.F on LEAVE.
Tamerton V
Tavistock

Tamerton Foliot to
TAVISTOCK
Third Class. Fare 1/10
The Passenger is requested to
see this ticket punched at the
time of issue

0544

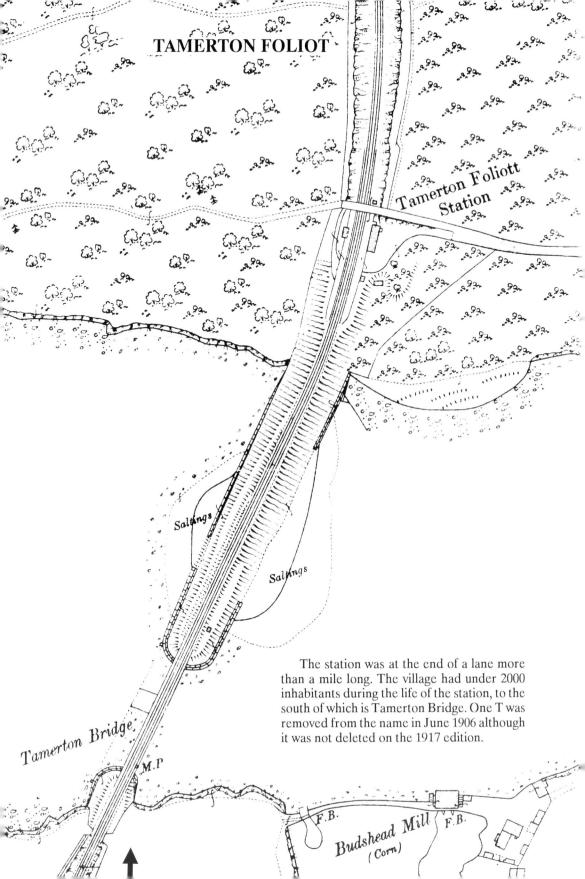

TAMERTON FOLIOT

Tamerton Foliott Station

Salángs

Salángs

The station was at the end of a lane more than a mile long. The village had under 2000 inhabitants during the life of the station, to the south of which is Tamerton Bridge. One T was removed from the name in June 1906 although it was not deleted on the 1917 edition.

Tamerton Bridge.

M.P

F.B.

Budshead Mill
(Corn)

F.B.

70. The porter waits optimistically for parcels. Goods by passenger trains were handled in the small shed on the right until 1956. The main building was still standing 40 years later. (Lens of Sutton)

→

71. A signal box was situated beyond the main building but it was only in use for a few years from 22nd December 1897, when the station opened. (Lens of Sutton)

TAMERTON FOLIOT	1928	1936
No. of passenger tickets issued	911	424
No. of season tickets issued	4	-
No. of passenger tickets collected	1243	482
No. of telegrams	50	-
No. of parcels forwarded	349	278
No. of parcels received	152	276
Horses forwarded	-	-
Milk forwarded - Cans 1928/Gallons 1936	-	-
Milk received - Cans 1928/Gallons 1936	-	-
General goods forwarded (tons)	6	4
General goods received (tons)	40	29
Coal, coke etc. received (tons)	-	-
Other minerals forwarded (tons)	-	-
Other minerals received (tons)	-	-
Trucks livestock forwarded	-	-
Trucks livestock received	-	-
Lavatory pennies	-	-

→

72. The station became a halt when staffing ceased on 5th January 1959. The cleanliness of the trains, their exhausts and the platforms steadily declined. The halt closed on 10th September 1962. (Lens of Sutton)

73. The route is within sight of the Tamar for almost two miles, much of it including views of I.K.Brunel's Royal Albert Bridge at Saltash. Running north on 31st March 1956 is class M7 0-4-4T no. 30035 with the 4.5pm Plymouth Friary to Brentor. (N.W.Sprinks)

74. Three locomotives were on the Royal Navy's Ernesettle Pier simultaneously when this picture was taken from an up train on the Royal Albert Bridge, sometime in November 1956. The pier also appears in the previous picture. The line was of 2ft 6ins gauge and passed under the main line in a tunnel. It closed in March 1980. (M.Daly)

75. Part of Ernesettle Pier is on the left and in the background is Ernesettle Admiralty Depot and sidings. These were laid in 1938 with a trailing connection from the down line. The 13.25 Plymouth to Gunnislake is running north (away from the camera) on 19th March 1981. The sidings were still in place in 1996 for use in a military emergency. (T.Heavyside)

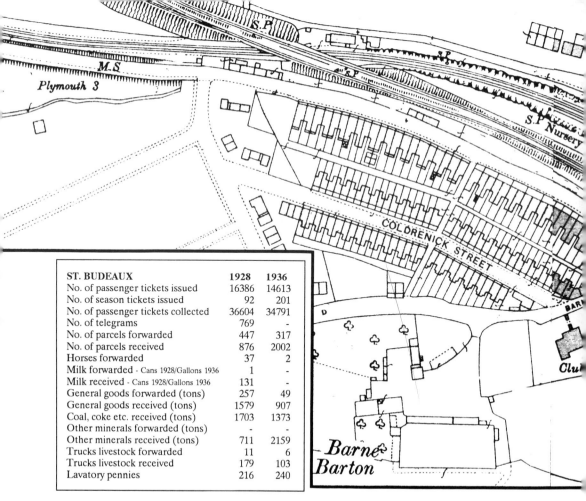

ST. BUDEAUX	1928	1936
No. of passenger tickets issued	16386	14613
No. of season tickets issued	92	201
No. of passenger tickets collected	36604	34791
No. of telegrams	769	-
No. of parcels forwarded	447	317
No. of parcels received	876	2002
Horses forwarded	37	2
Milk forwarded - Cans 1928/Gallons 1936	1	-
Milk received - Cans 1928/Gallons 1936	131	-
General goods forwarded (tons)	257	49
General goods received (tons)	1579	907
Coal, coke etc. received (tons)	1703	1373
Other minerals forwarded (tons)	-	-
Other minerals received (tons)	711	2159
Trucks livestock forwarded	11	6
Trucks livestock received	179	103
Lavatory pennies	216	240

76.   A postcard franked in 1906 reveals that only the down side path was covered, this being for the benefit of passengers queuing for tickets. The population was only 2470 in 1891 but residential development was rapid thereafter. (M.Dart coll.)

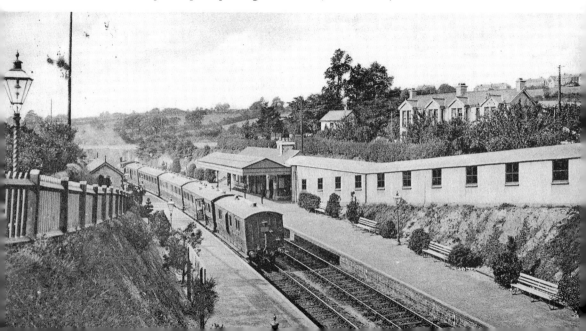

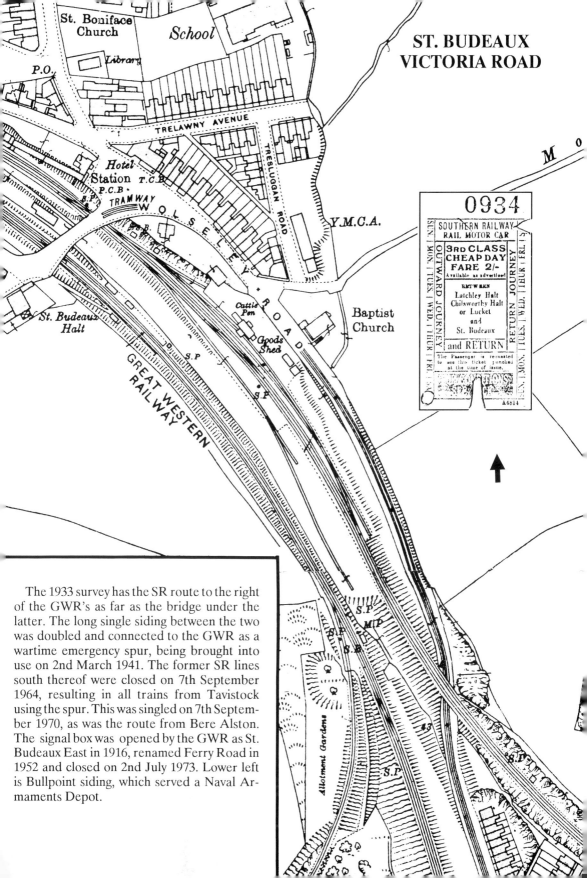

ST. BUDEAUX
VICTORIA ROAD

St. Boniface Church
School
Library
P.O.
Trelawny Avenue
Hotel
Station T.C.B.
P.C.B.
S.P.
TRAMWAY
WOLSELEY
ROAD
TRESLUGGAN ROAD
Y.M.C.A.
St. Budeaux Halt
GREAT WESTERN RAILWAY
Cattle Pen
Goods Shed
S.P.
S.P.
Baptist Church

0934

SOUTHERN RAILWAY
RAIL MOTOR CAR
3RD CLASS
CHEAP DAY
FARE 2/-
Available as advertised
BETWEEN
Latchley Halt
Chilsworthy Halt
or Lucket
and
St. Budeaux
and RETURN
The Passenger is requested
to see this ticket punched
at the time of issue.
A4814
SUN. | MON. | TUES. | WED. | THUR | FRI.
OUTWARD JOURNEY
RETURN JOURNEY
SUN. | MON. | TUES. | WED. | THUR | FRI.

Allotment Gardens
S.P.
S.P.
S.P.
M.P.
S.P.
43
S.P.

The 1933 survey has the SR route to the right of the GWR's as far as the bridge under the latter. The long single siding between the two was doubled and connected to the GWR as a wartime emergency spur, being brought into use on 2nd March 1941. The former SR lines south thereof were closed on 7th September 1964, resulting in all trains from Tavistock using the spur. This was singled on 7th September 1970, as was the route from Bere Alston. The signal box was opened by the GWR as St. Budeaux East in 1916, renamed Ferry Road in 1952 and closed on 2nd July 1973. Lower left is Bullpoint siding, which served a Naval Armaments Depot.

77. Most of Plymouth's street tramways were electrified by 1901 and, in an attempt to regain lost traffic, the LSWR started an almost hourly motor train service between here and Ply- mouth Friary. Class T1 no. 359 terminates the 4.35pm from that station on 12th May 1939. It was not fitted for push-pull working and so is about to run round. (J.R.W.Kirkby)

78. A northwestward view in the 1950s shows the light coloured bridge and platforms of the Western Region Ferry Road station and the darker structures of the Southern Region Vic- toria Road station. The 1941 connection is in the centre and proceeding towards Devonport is no. 34023 *Blackmore Vale*. (M.Daly)

ST BUDEAUX
FERRY ROAD
WESTERN REGION
← 50 YARDS LEFT

ST BUDEAUX·VICTORIA ROAD
(SOUTHERN REGION)
TICKET OFFICE FOR
TAVISTOCK, OKEHAMPTON, EXETER
AND ALL STATIONS TO WATERLOO

FOR
DIRECT SERVICES
INTO
SOUTH CORNWALL

CHANGE AT

| BERE ALSTON
FOR
CALLINGTON
BRANCH LINE | OKEHAMPTON
FOR
NORTH CORNWALL
LINE | YEOFORD
FOR
NORTH DEVON
LINE |

79. The suffix "Victoria Road" was added on 26th September 1949 and "Halt" was applied between 18th July 1965 (when staffing ceased) and 5th May 1969. (R.M.Casserley coll.)

80. Class N 2-6-0 no. 31834 runs over the points of the connecting spur with the 10.2am Plymouth to Waterloo on 28th June 1962. The signal box closed on 25th July 1965 but the goods yard had ceased to handle traffic on 11th December 1961. This box replaced one destroyed by bombs in March 1941. (J.J.Smith)

81. Looking towards Plymouth in 1962, it is evident that the two lines of the connection between the two systems were not parallel. In the distance is the ex-GWR Ferry Road box. No. D2176 is working four wagons from the Dockyard via Keyham to Devonport Kings Road. The two brake vans facilitated reversal at Victoria Road. (J.J.Smith)

82. Only the final portion of the long covered way remained when the platforms were photographed on 14th December 1963. Two halts were opened south of the station in 1906; Weston Mill Halt, which closed on 14th September 1921 and Camels Head Halt (named after a nearby public house) which lasted until 4th May 1942. (C.L.Caddy coll.)

83. The 12.09 from Gunnislake calls at the one remaining platform on 19th March 1981. The sign above the shelter reads STOP END OF ONE TRAIN WORKING. There is a cabinet on the platform containing the staff apparatus, which is released from Plymouth panel. (T.Heavyside)

84. The driver of the 10.20 from Gunnislake replaces the staff on 18th March 1995. In the distance is the only signal on the branch and beyond it is a crossover on the main line for use by down branch trains. (V.Mitchell)

85. A down train of spent ballast has crossed Weston Mill viaduct behind no. D1035 *Western Yeoman* on 31st May 1973. The former SR route ran diagonally across the top left part of the picture. (G.Gillham)

FORD (DEVON)

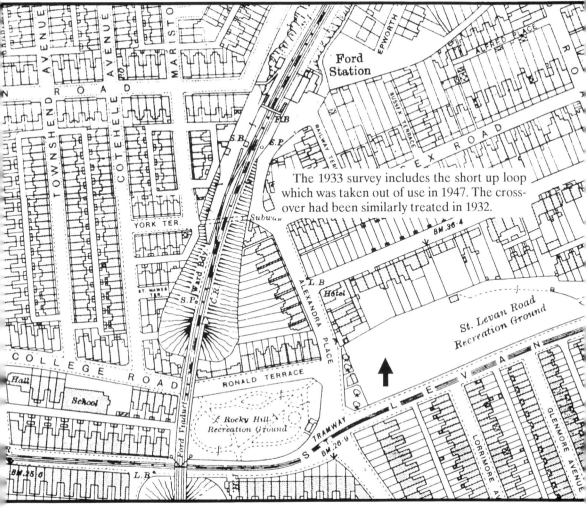

The 1933 survey includes the short up loop which was taken out of use in 1947. The crossover had been similarly treated in 1932.

86. A northward view includes the original timber footbridge and a fall-face ground signal. There was an inclined pathway from the road located between the up shelter and the footbridge steps. (Lens of Sutton)

FORD	1928	1936
No. of passenger tickets issued	21950	19898
No. of season tickets issued	152	317
No. of passenger tickets collected	32135	40848
No. of telegrams	-	-
No. of parcels forwarded	305	214
No. of parcels received	853	1212
Horses forwarded	-	-
Milk forwarded - Cans 1928/Gallons 1936	-	-
Milk received - Cans 1928/Gallons 1936	2434	39933
General goods forwarded (tons)	-	-
General goods received (tons)	8	-
Coal, coke etc. received (tons)	2291	-
Other minerals forwarded (tons)	-	-
Other minerals received (tons)	-	-
Trucks livestock forwarded	-	-
Trucks livestock received	-	-
Lavatory pennies	264	380

87.   Class T9 no. 715 approaches Ford Viaduct with the 8.46am Exeter Central to Plymouth Friary on 23rd May 1935. Tall domestic wireless aerials are also evident. The limestone faced concrete viaduct was demolished in 1988. (H.C.Casserley)

88.   A southward snap reveals that the LSWR footbridge had been replaced by an SR standard concrete structure. These were prefabricated at their concrete works at Exmouth Junction. Goods by passenger train were handled until 1st September 1952.
(Lens of Sutton)

89.   The boarded-up buildings were photographed in 1966. They were closed with the line on 7th September 1964. The signal box at the south end of the up platform was shut on 2nd March 1947. Albert Road Halt was nearly one mile to the south and was situated between the 374 yd long Ford Tunnel and Devonport Park Tunnel, which was 530 yds in length. The halt was in use from 1st November 1906 until 13th January 1947. (C.L.Caddy coll.)

DEVONPORT KINGS ROAD

Our route turns from a southerly to an easterly direction under Devonport Park, as indicated on this 1934 survey. The single line at the bottom of the map is to Stonehouse Pool. The crane marked was of 10-ton capacity.

DEVONPORT	1928	1936
No. of passenger tickets issued	63067	47101
No. of season tickets issued	182	147
No. of passenger tickets collected	100563	84531
No. of telegrams	6421	8710
No. of parcels forwarded	3615	4580
No. of parcels received	15975	17714
Horses forwarded	163	94
Milk forwarded - Cans 1928/Gallons 1936	7	67
Milk received - Cans 1928/Gallons 1936	10747	52357
General goods forwarded (tons)	-	5291
General goods received (tons)	-	15999
Coal, coke etc. received (tons)	-	7455
Other minerals forwarded (tons)	-	4620
Other minerals received (tons)	-	3940
Trucks livestock forwarded	-	6
Trucks livestock received	-	415
Lavatory pennies	10188	5580

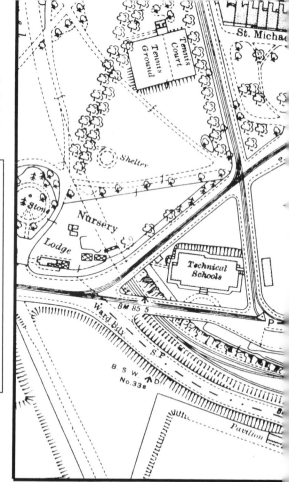

90. The main entrance was on the north side and was intended to be impressive. It served as a terminal station from 17th May 1876 until 2nd June 1890, trains arriving from Waterloo from the east. (Lens of Sutton)

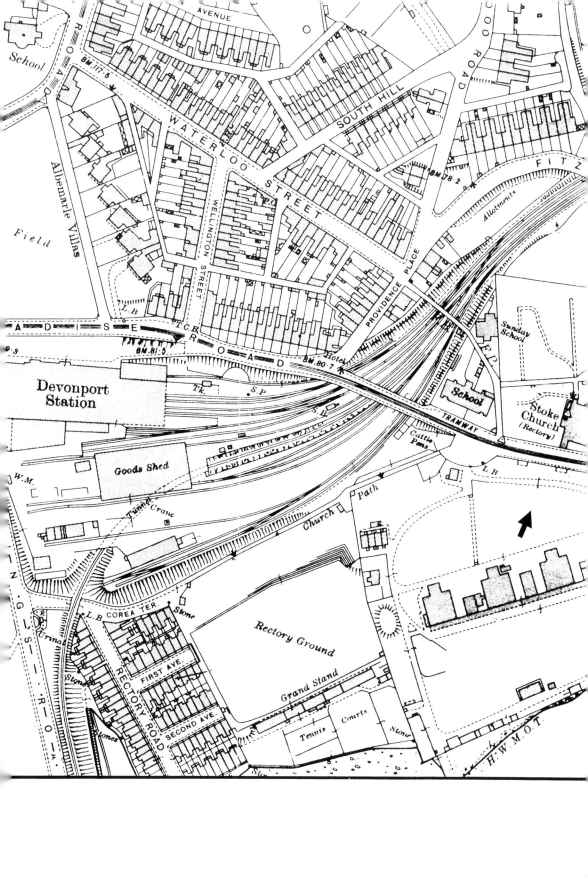

91.   It appears that the station was designed for through services, although some accounts state that the west wall was pierced in 1890. This is it, long before the devastation of World War II. (Lens of Sutton)

92.   Enemy action destroyed the fine overall roof necessitating the provision of platform canopies. This is the down platform in 1945, looking towards Ford. The suffix "Kings Road" was added on 26th September 1949. (H.C.Casserley)

93. Class M7 no. 35 approaches the up platform on 30th August 1945 with the 1.22pm Plymouth Friary to Tavistock. Note the outdated name of the hotel, which was still so named in 1996. (H.C.Casserley)

94. A down freight passes through on 28th June 1962 behind class N 2-6-0 no. 31849. Compare this photograph with no. 92. The clock tower is not on the railway premises, but on a place of further education. (J.J.Smith)

95. The spacious platforms were heavily used by Naval personnel and their kit. Note that there is a refreshment room on the up side. Having survived the ravages of war, the fine buildings were destroyed in favour of modern creations for technical instruction. (J.J.Smith)

96. The LSWR engine shed was closed in 1909 and photographed in 1964, it having been used for mineral water production in the interim. The camera was near the site of the turntable, the boundary of the pit of which shows on the map. (S.C.Nash)

97. Class 42 no. D824 stands with the 11.30am Brighton to Plymouth train on 1st August 1964. The water tank behind the locomotive appears on the left of the previous picture. (S.C.Nash)

98. A May 1964 panorama includes the Stonehouse Pool line (last used in 1966) passing under the goods shed and a Brighton-bound train. The signal box closed on 14th February 1963; the station followed on 7th September 1964 but the goods yard remained in use until 4th January 1971. (A.Jeffery)

PLYMOUTH NORTH ROAD

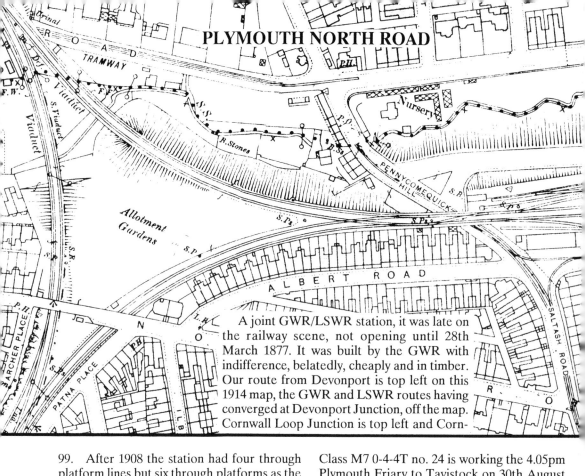

A joint GWR/LSWR station, it was late on the railway scene, not opening until 28th March 1877. It was built by the GWR with indifference, belatedly, cheaply and in timber. Our route from Devonport is top left on this 1914 map, the GWR and LSWR routes having converged at Devonport Junction, off the map. Cornwall Loop Junction is top left and Corn-

99. After 1908 the station had four through platform lines but six through platforms as the outer two tracks each had two faces. On the left is no. 3, which was the down island platform.

Class M7 0-4-4T no. 24 is working the 4.05pm Plymouth Friary to Tavistock on 30th August 1945. (H.C.Casserley)

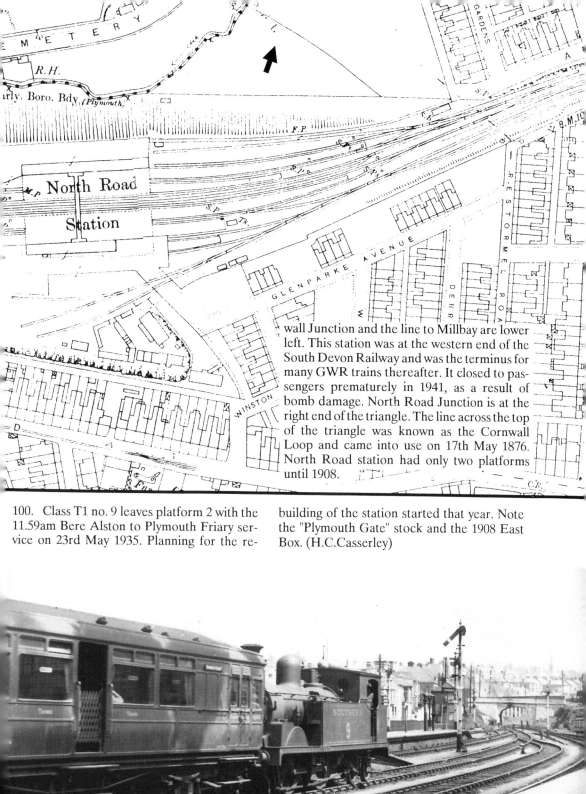

wall Junction and the line to Millbay are lower left. This station was at the western end of the South Devon Railway and was the terminus for many GWR trains thereafter. It closed to passengers prematurely in 1941, as a result of bomb damage. North Road Junction is at the right end of the triangle. The line across the top of the triangle was known as the Cornwall Loop and came into use on 17th May 1876. North Road station had only two platforms until 1908.

100. Class T1 no. 9 leaves platform 2 with the 11.59am Bere Alston to Plymouth Friary service on 23rd May 1935. Planning for the rebuilding of the station started that year. Note the "Plymouth Gate" stock and the 1908 East Box. (H.C.Casserley)

101. The mean timber structure was inappropriate to serve as the city's main and, eventually, only station. Rebuilding started in 1938, recommenced after the war in 1956 and was completed in 1962. The suffix "North" was in use until 14th September 1958. (Lens of Sutton)

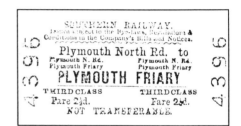

103. The stone arch seen in picture 100 was replaced with three concrete spans in 1938. Nearby is East Box which was in use from 25th June 1939 until 26th November 1960. Colour light signals are ready for commissioning as no. 41317 proceeds to Tavistock North on 14th May 1960. (M.Dart)

102. Widening of the road bridge west of the station involved moving the 1904 West Box bodily northwards in January 1938. Seven through platforms and four parcel docks were created. West Box is on the right of this July 1956 westward view. (R.C.Riley)

104.   Class N 2-6-0 no. 31834 waits to leave from platform 2 with the 10-02am to Okehampton on 3rd April 1964. Ten years later, the centre parts of the through lines at platforms 2 and 3 were removed and four bay platforms were formed, only the western part of no. 3 being used for passengers. (L.W.Rowe)

105.   At platform 3 on 29th March 1982 is the 13.15 for Gunnislake. The pitched roof in the background covers the walkway built between the old platforms 2 and 3 in 1974. (J.Scrace)

106.   Gunnislake trains use platform 3, as witnessed on 18th March 1995. There was no renumbering in 1974 and so there were no platforms numbered 1 or 2 subsequently. On the left is dock 4. The lines at docks 1 and 2 were removed in 1975. (V.Mitchell)

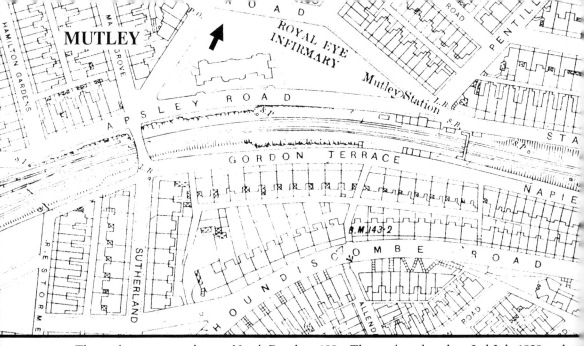

MUTLEY

The station was very close to North Road, the sidings on the left of this map being those on the right of the previous one.

108. The station closed on 3rd July 1939 and — part of the up (GWR designation) platform was removed to allow extension of some of the North Road sidings. (M.Dart coll.)

107. The station predates North Road, having opened over five years earlier on 1st August 1871. The signal box near the group on the left had closed by 1896. This is an eastward view. The GWR and LSWR had their own booking offices for a period. (Lens of Sutton)

109. No. 34024 *Tamar Valley* emerges from — the west end of the 183yd long Mutley Tunnel on 14th May 1956, bound for Okehampton. The bore was completed in 1849. Lipson Vale Halt was situated east of the tunnel and was in use from 1st June 1904 until 22nd March 1942. (M.Dart)

The 6 ins to 1 mile map of 1938 has our route from North Road to Friary curving from the top left to lower left borders. The GWR locomotive depot is within the triangular junction.

110. No. 34063 *229 Squadron* runs south on Lipson No. 1 Curve on its way to Plymouth Friary in the 1950s. The curve was opened on 1st April 1891, three months before passenger services started. The former GWR Laira Shed is in the background. (M.Daly)

111. A southward view of Mount Gold Junction on 28th June 1962 shows empty coaches from the Friary sidings bound for North Road via the curve on the right. The signal box (centre) was in use from 1891 to 10th November 1973. The path on the left is bounded by the rails of the 4ft 6ins gauge horse worked Plymouth & Dartmoor Railway (Lee Moor Tramway from 1854) which conveyed mineral traffic regularly until 1947. (J.J.Smith)

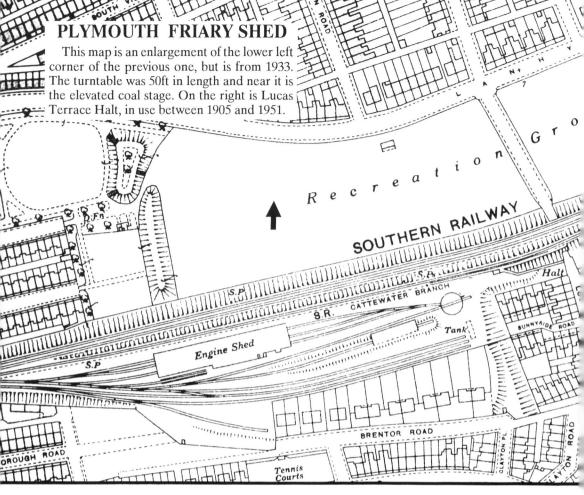

PLYMOUTH FRIARY SHED

This map is an enlargement of the lower left corner of the previous one, but is from 1933. The turntable was 50ft in length and near it is the elevated coal stage. On the right is Lucas Terrace Halt, in use between 1905 and 1951.

Recreation Gro

SOUTHERN RAILWAY

S.R. CATTEWATER BRANCH

Engine Shed

Tank

S.P

Halt

BUNNYSIDE ROAD

BRENTOR ROAD

CLAYTON PL

CLAYTON ROAD

OROUGH ROAD

Tennis Courts

112. The PDSWJR's three locomotives were LSWR property for only one year, 1922. Their 1907 Hawthorn Leslie 0-6-0 was recorded out- side the shed on 15th August 1923, by which time it was in SR ownership. (H.C.Casserley)

113. The shed replaced a small one (located near the station and shown on the next map) in about 1908. It was usually allocated about 25 engines and was damaged several times during the bombing. (Lens of Sutton)

114. A photograph from 19th June 1950 shows typical locomotives of the era - a Bulleid Light Pacific for main line work, an ex-PDSWJR 0-6-2T for the Callington branch, a B4 class 0-4-0T for dock shunting and an O2 for local services. The shed closed in May 1963 and the remaining locomotives moved to Laira. (J.J.Smith)

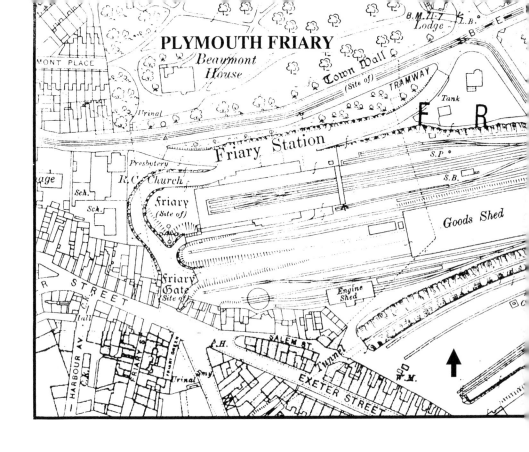

115. The entrance was on the north side of the station and is seen in 1913. The station opened on 1st July 1891 and provided the fastest service to London for many years. (R.M.Casserley coll.)

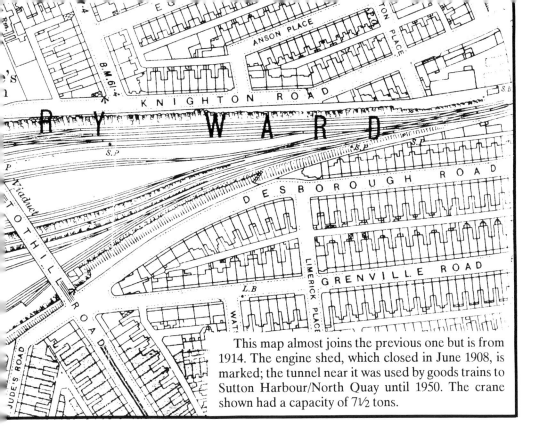

This map almost joins the previous one but is from 1914. The engine shed, which closed in June 1908, is marked; the tunnel near it was used by goods trains to Sutton Harbour/North Quay until 1950. The crane shown had a capacity of 7½ tons.

116. The building that we have just admired is to the right of the footbridge, an unusual feature at a terminal station. Class T1 0-4-4T no. 72 is about to leave for Tavistock on 8th July 1924. On the left is no. 218, a class O2 0-4-4T. Also featured is "B" Box, which was in use until 21st July 1962. (H.C.Casserley)

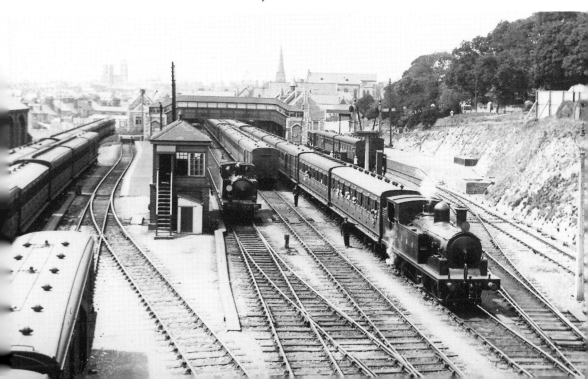

117. The running lines are beyond the signal in this northward view of the area marked WARD on the map. The assorted rolling stock is worthy of close study, as is the 1908 class B4 0-4-0T no. 82 shunting on 14th June 1926. (H.C.Casserley)

118. An eastward view from Tothill Road bridge in July 1957 includes a local train departing and "A" Box, which closed on 24th April 1966. Passenger services ceased here on 15th September 1958. The locomotive in the distance is near the engine shed. (D.Cullum)

119.   Freight services were concentrated at
Friary and the former passenger lines were
used for empty wagon storage. Most of the
former LSWR structures were still extant in
September 1965, the footbridge and signals
being the main losses. (C.L.Caddy)

120.   Tothill Road bridge finally comes into
view as we watch no. 08953 *Plymouth* and no.
08839 shunting on 17th February 1983. Only
two tracks were in use in 1996 (for run round
purposes) and the land beyond the bridge had
been developed for commercial and residential purposes. (D.Mitchell)

MP Middleton Press

Easebourne Lane, Midhurst, West Sussex. GU29 9AZ Tel: 01730 813169 Fax: 01730 812601
If books are not available from your local transport stockist, order direct with cheque, Visa or Mastercard, post free UK.

BRANCH LINES
Branch Line to Allhallows
Branch Lines around Ascot
Branch Line to Ashburton
Branch Lines around Bodmin
Branch Line to Bude
Branch Lines around Canterbury
Branch Lines around Chard & Yeovil
Branch Line to Cheddar
Branch Lines around Cromer
Branch Lines to Effingham Junction
Branch Lines around Exmouth
Branch Line to Fairford
Branch Line to Hawkhurst
Branch Line to Hayling
Branch Lines to Horsham
Branch Line to Ilfracombe
Branch Line to Kingswear
Branch Lines to Launceston & Princetown
Branch Lines to Longmoor
Branch Line to Looe
Branch Line to Lyme Regis
Branch Lines around March
Branch Lines around Midhurst
Branch Line to Minehead
Branch Line to Moretonhampstead
Branch Lines to Newport (IOW)
Branch Line to Padstow
Branch Lines around Plymouth
Branch Line to Selsey
Branch Lines around Sheerness
Branch Line to Swanage *updated*
Branch Line to Tenterden
Branch Lines to Torrington
Branch Lines to Tunbridge Wells
Branch Line to Upwell
Branch Lines around Weymouth
Branch Lines around Wimborne
Branch Lines around Wisbech

NARROW GAUGE BRANCH LINES
Branch Line to Lynton
Branch Lines around Portmadoc 1923-46
Branch Lines around Porthmadog 1954-94
Two-Foot Gauge Survivors
Romneyrail

SOUTH COAST RAILWAYS
Ashford to Dover
Brighton to Eastbourne
Chichester to Portsmouth
Dover to Ramsgate
Eastbourne to Hastings
Hastings to Ashford
Portsmouth to Southampton
Southampton to Bournemouth
Worthing to Chichester

SOUTHERN MAIN LINES
Bromley South to Rochester
Charing Cross to Orpington
Crawley to Littlehampton
Dartford to Sittingbourne
East Croydon to Three Bridges
Epsom to Horsham
Exeter to Barnstaple
Exeter to Tavistock
Faversham to Dover
London Bridge to East Croydon
Orpington to Tonbridge
Salisbury to Yeovil

Swanley to Ashford
Tavistock to Plymouth
Victoria to East Croydon
Waterloo to Windsor
Waterloo to Woking
Woking to Portsmouth
Woking to Southampton
Yeovil to Exeter

EASTERN MAIN LINES
Fenchurch Street to Barking

COUNTRY RAILWAY ROUTES
Andover to Southampton
Bournemouth to Evercreech Jn.
Burnham to Evercreech Junction
Croydon to East Grinstead
Didcot to Winchester
Fareham to Salisbury
Frome to Bristol
Guildford to Redhill
Porthmadog to Blaenau
Reading to Basingstoke
Reading to Guildford
Redhill to Ashford
Salisbury to Westbury
Stratford Upon Avon to Cheltenham
Strood to Paddock Wood
Taunton to Barnstaple
Wenford Bridge to Fowey
Westbury to Bath
Woking to Alton
Yeovil to Dorchester

GREAT RAILWAY ERAS
Ashford from Steam to Eurostar
Clapham Junction 50 years of change
Festiniog in the Fifties
Festiniog in the Sixties
Isle of Wight Lines 50 years of change
Railways to Victory 1944-46

LONDON SUBURBAN RAILWAYS
Caterham and Tattenham Corner
Charing Cross to Dartford
Clapham Jn. to Beckenham Jn.
East London Line
Finsbury Park to Alexandra Palace
Holborn Viaduct to Lewisham
Kingston and Hounslow Loops
Lewisham to Dartford
Lines around Wimbledon
London Bridge to Addiscombe
North London Line
South London Line
West Croydon to Epsom
West London Line
Willesden Junction to Richmond
Wimbledon to Epsom

STEAMING THROUGH
Steaming through Cornwall
Steaming through the Isle of Wight
Steaming through Kent
Steaming through West Hants
Steaming through West Sussex

TRAMWAY CLASSICS
Aldgate & Stepney Tramways
Barnet & Finchley Tramways
Bath Tramways

Bournemouth & Poole Tramways
Brighton's Tramways
Camberwell & W.Norwood Tramways
Clapham & Streatham Tramways
Dover's Tramways
East Ham & West Ham Tramways
Edgware and Willesden Tramways
Eltham & Woolwich Tramways
Embankment & Waterloo Tramways
Enfield & Wood Green Tramways
Exeter & Taunton Tramways
Gosport & Horndean Tramways
Greenwich & Dartford Tramways
Hampstead & Highgate Tramways
Hastings Tramways
Holborn & Finsbury Tramways
Ilford & Barking Tramways
Kingston & Wimbledon Tramways
Lewisham & Catford Tramways
Liverpool Tramways 1. Eastern Routes
Liverpool Tramways 2. Southern Routes
Maidstone & Chatham Tramways
North Kent Tramways
Portsmouth's Tramways
Reading Tramways
Seaton & Eastbourne Tramways
Shepherds Bush & Uxbridge Tramways
Southampton Tramways
Southend-on-sea Tramways
Southwark & Deptford Tramways
Stamford Hill Tramways
Thanet's Tramways
Victoria & Lambeth Tramways
Waltham Cross & Edmonton Tramways
Walthamstow & Leyton Tramways
Wandsworth & Battersea Tramways

TROLLEYBUS CLASSICS
Croydon Trolleybuses
Bournemouth Trolleybuses
Hastings Trolleybuses
Maidstone Trolleybuses
Reading Trolleybuses
Woolwich & Dartford Trolleybuses

WATERWAY ALBUMS
Kent and East Sussex Waterways
London to Portsmouth Waterway
Surrey Waterways
West Sussex Waterways

MILITARY BOOKS and VIDEO
Battle over Portsmouth
Battle over Sussex 1940
Blitz over Sussex 1941-42
Bombers over Sussex 1943-45
Bognor at War
Military Defence of West Sussex
Secret Sussex Resistance
Sussex Home Guard
War on the Line
War on the Line VIDEO

OTHER BOOKS and VIDEO
Betwixt Petersfield & Midhurst
Changing Midhurst
East Grinstead Then & Now
Garraway Father & Son
Index to all Stations
South Eastern & Chatham Railways
London Chatham & Dover Railway